The Room on the Broom Song

D1323515

A Song based on ROOM ON THE BROOM

by Julia Donaldson Illustrated by Axel Scheffler

MACMILLAN CHILDREN'S BOOKS

I am a cat, as lean as can be.
Is there room on the broom for a cat like me?

Yes, yes, yes!

I am a dog, as keen as can be.
Is there room on the broom for a dog like me?

Yes, yes, yes!

I am a bird, as green as can be.
Is there room on the broom for a bird like me?

Yes, yes, yes!

I am a frog, as clean as can be.
Is there room on the broom for a frog like me?

Yes, yes . . .

No!

I am a dragon, as mean as can be.
Is there room on the broom
for a dragon like me?

No, no, no! Off you go!

Ho-ho-ho, ho-ho-ho, ho!

The Room on the Broom Song
by Julia Donaldson

G   **E dim 7**   **A min**   **D**

I am a cat, as lean as can be. Is there
I am a dog, as keen as can be. Is there
I am a bird, as green as can be. Is there
I am a frog, as clean as can be. Is there

G   **E min**   **A7**   **D**   **G**   **D**   **G**

room on the broom for a cat like me? Yes, yes, yes!
room on the broom for a dog like me? Yes, yes, yes!
room on the broom for a bird like me? Yes, yes, yes!
room on the broom for a frog like me? Yes, yes... no!

G   **E dim 7**   **A min**   **D**

I am a dra – gon, as mean as can be. Is there

G   **E min**   **A7**   **D**   **G**   **D**   **G**

room on the broom for a dra–gon like me? No, no, no!

C   **D**   **G**   **D**   **G**

Off you go! Ho – ho – ho ho – ho – ho HO!